AF409224

Social Media Madness: How to Maintain Your Sanity in a Digital World

C. P. Kumar
Reiki Healer
Roorkee - 247667, India

Copyright © 2023 C. P. Kumar

All rights reserved.

No part of this book may be reproduced or transmitted in any form or by any means, electronic or mechanical, including photocopying, recording, or by any information storage and retrieval system, without permission in writing from the author.

DEDICATION

To everyone who has ever felt overwhelmed or consumed by the never-ending stream of social media, this book is dedicated to you. May it serve as a reminder that your mental health and well-being should always come first, and that finding a balance in the digital world is possible.

C. P. Kumar

CONTENTS

PREFACE

Social media has become an integral part of our lives, shaping the way we communicate, connect, and consume information. However, this digital world has also brought with it a set of challenges and risks that can impact our mental health and overall well-being.

This book, "Social Media Madness: How to Maintain Your Sanity in a Digital World," aims to provide a comprehensive guide to navigating the world of social media while preserving your mental health and personal boundaries. It will delve into the dark side of social media, exploring its impact on mental health and addiction, and offer practical tips on how to cope with FOMO and comparison envy.

The book will also emphasize the importance of mindful social media use, highlighting the benefits of building and maintaining positive relationships online and identifying and combating cyberbullying and online harassment. It will also discuss ways to protect your privacy and security on social media and the significance of finding balance and setting boundaries.

Furthermore, the book will explore the benefits of disconnecting from social media and the importance of taking breaks to reconnect with the real world. It will also provide best practices and etiquette for navigating social media in the workplace.

Whether you are a social media enthusiast, a concerned parent, or a professional navigating the digital world, this book is a must-read for anyone looking to maintain their sanity and well-being in a world dominated by social media.

C. P. Kumar

Reiki Healer

Former Scientist 'G', National Institute of Hydrology

Roorkee - 247667, India

E-mail: cpkumar@yahoo.com

Web: https://www.angelfire.com/nh/cpkumar/virgo.html

Introduction

Social media has revolutionized the way people interact with each other and the world. The ability to connect with people from all over the world and share information instantly has transformed the way we communicate, learn, and entertain ourselves. However, social media has also given rise to a new phenomenon - Social Media Madness. In this article, we will explore the concept of Social Media Madness and its impact on our society.

What is Social Media Madness?

Social Media Madness refers to the excessive use of social media platforms, leading to addiction and negative consequences. It is a term used to describe the compulsive behavior of individuals who spend hours on social media, scrolling through their feeds, liking posts, and commenting on updates. Social Media Madness can be identified by the following characteristics:

- ❖ Spending excessive amounts of time on social media platforms
- ❖ Neglecting other responsibilities or relationships due to social media use
- ❖ Feeling anxious or irritable when unable to access social media
- ❖ Obsessively checking for updates, likes, and comments
- ❖ Constantly comparing oneself to others on social media
- ❖ Feeling a sense of validation and self-worth based on social media engagement

Social Media Madness is not limited to any particular age group or demographic. It can affect anyone who uses social media, regardless of their age, gender, or background.

Causes of Social Media Madness

Several factors contribute to Social Media Madness, including:

1. FOMO (Fear of Missing Out)

FOMO is a common phenomenon experienced by social media users who feel anxious about missing out on social events, news, or updates. The constant need to stay connected and up-to-date can lead to compulsive social media use.

2. Dopamine Addiction

Social media platforms are designed to trigger dopamine release in our brains, leading to a sense of pleasure and satisfaction. The constant validation and reward system of social media can lead to addiction and compulsive behavior.

3. Social Comparison

Social media is a platform for people to showcase their achievements, experiences, and lifestyles. The constant exposure to other people's lives can lead to social comparison and feelings of inadequacy or insecurity.

4. Algorithmic Design

Social media algorithms are designed to show users content that is most likely to keep them engaged. This personalized content can lead to a filter bubble, where users are exposed to information and opinions that reinforce their existing beliefs and biases.

Impact of Social Media Madness

Social Media Madness has several negative consequences, including:

1. Mental Health Issues

Compulsive social media use can lead to anxiety, depression, and other mental health issues. The constant comparison and validation-seeking behavior can lead to low self-esteem and feelings of inadequacy.

2. Relationship Problems

Neglecting real-life relationships due to social media use can lead to relationship problems and even breakups. The constant need for social media validation can also strain existing relationships.

3. Productivity Loss

Excessive social media use can lead to a loss of productivity and reduced performance at work or school.

Spending hours on social media can lead to physical health issues such as eye strain, neck pain, and insomnia.

Social media platforms have become a breeding ground for misinformation and fake news. The algorithmic design of social media can reinforce existing biases and lead to the spread of misinformation.

How to Overcome Social Media Madness

Here are some ways to overcome Social Media Madness:

1. Set Limits

Set limits on your social media use. Decide on a specific amount of time you will spend on social media each day and stick to it.

2. Take Breaks

Take regular breaks from social media. Go for a walk, read a book, or engage in other offline activities.

3. Seek Support

If you feel like you cannot control your social media use, seek support from friends, family, or a mental health professional. They can provide guidance and support to help you overcome Social Media Madness.

4. Practice Mindfulness

Practice mindfulness techniques such as meditation or deep breathing to reduce anxiety and stress related to social media use.

5. Focus on Real-Life Relationships

Focus on building and maintaining real-life relationships. Make an effort to spend time with friends and family, engage in activities outside of social media, and build meaningful connections.

Be aware of the algorithmic design of social media platforms and the impact it can have on your beliefs and opinions. Seek out diverse sources of information to avoid being trapped in a filter bubble.

Challenge social comparison by recognizing that social media is not a realistic representation of people's lives. Practice gratitude and focus on your own accomplishments and experiences rather than comparing yourself to others.

Conclusion

Social Media Madness is a growing phenomenon that can have negative consequences on our mental and physical health, relationships, and productivity. It is important to recognize the signs of Social Media Madness and take steps to overcome it. By setting limits, taking breaks, seeking support, practicing mindfulness, focusing on real-life relationships, being aware of algorithmic design, and challenging social comparison, we can overcome Social Media

Madness and use social media in a healthy
and positive way.

Introduction

Social media has become an integral part of our daily lives, connecting us to friends, family, and the world at large. However, the rise of social media has also brought with it some negative consequences, particularly in terms of its impact on mental health. In this article, we will explore the dark side of social media, its impact on mental health, and what we can do to mitigate its negative effects.

Comparison and Self-Esteem

One of the most common negative effects of social media is the impact it has on our self-esteem. Social media platforms are often used to showcase the highlights of one's life, which can lead to unrealistic comparisons and feelings of inadequacy. Seeing other people's seemingly perfect lives can cause us to question our own accomplishments, making us feel inferior and insecure.

Furthermore, social media provides an opportunity for others to comment and share their opinions. Negative feedback and comments can further erode our self-esteem, leading to a range of mental health issues, including anxiety and depression.

Addiction and Dependence

Social media addiction is another serious problem that can have a significant impact on mental health. Social media platforms are designed to keep users engaged for as long as possible, and this can lead to a compulsion to check notifications and update feeds. The constant need to check social media can become an addiction, leading to a range of mental health problems, including anxiety, depression, and social isolation.

Sleep Disorders

Social media can also disrupt our sleep patterns, leading to a range of sleep disorders. The blue light emitted by screens can interfere with our circadian rhythms, making it harder to fall asleep and stay asleep. This can lead to a range of sleep disorders, including insomnia and sleep apnea. Poor sleep can have a negative impact on mental health, leading to a range of issues, including anxiety and depression.

Cyberbullying

Social media provides a platform for cyberbullying, which can have a devastating impact on mental health. Cyberbullying can take many forms, including harassment, abuse, and the spread of rumors and lies. Victims of cyberbullying can experience a range of mental health issues, including anxiety, depression, and suicidal thoughts.

Negative Social Comparisons

Another negative effect of social media is the impact it has on our relationships. Social media provides a platform for negative social comparisons, which can lead to jealousy and envy. Seeing other people's seemingly perfect lives can make us feel inadequate, leading to resentment and bitterness towards our friends and family. This can damage our relationships and lead to feelings of loneliness and isolation.

What Can We Do?

While social media can have a negative impact on mental health, there are steps we can take to mitigate its negative effects. Here are some strategies that can help:

1. Limit Your Time on Social Media

Limiting your time on social media can help reduce the negative impact it has on your mental health. Consider setting aside specific times each day to check your accounts, and avoid using social media during the hours leading up to bedtime.

2. Unfollow or Mute Negative Accounts

Unfollowing or muting accounts that trigger negative emotions can also be helpful. If certain accounts or people make you feel inadequate or upset, consider removing them from your feed.

3. Focus on Real-Life Connections

Focusing on real-life connections with friends and family can also help reduce the negative impact of social media. Spending time with loved ones in person can help improve your mood and reduce feelings of loneliness and isolation.

4. Practice Self-Care

Finally, practicing self-care can help improve your mental health and reduce the negative impact of social media. Engage in activities that make you feel good, such as exercise, meditation, or reading. Taking care of yourself can help you feel more confident and resilient, reducing the impact of negative social comparisons.

Conclusion

Social media can have a negative impact on our mental health, particularly in terms of comparison and self-esteem, addiction and dependence, sleep disorders, cyberbullying, and negative social comparisons. However, there are steps we can take to mitigate these negative effects, including limiting our time on social media, unfollowing or muting negative accounts, focusing on real-life connections, and practicing self-care.

It's essential to remember that social media is a tool, and we have control over how we use it. We can choose to use social media in a way that benefits our mental health and well-being, or we can allow it to control us and contribute to negative mental health outcomes. By being mindful of our social media use and taking steps to protect our mental health, we can enjoy the benefits of social media while minimizing its negative effects.

Introduction

Social media has become an integral part of our daily lives. It has transformed the way we communicate, interact and share information. While social media has many benefits, it can also be addictive. Social media addiction is a growing concern worldwide, and it affects people of all ages. This article aims to discuss the signs and symptoms of social media addiction and how it can be managed.

What is Social Media Addiction?

Social media addiction refers to the excessive use of social media platforms that interferes with a person's daily life. People who are addicted to social media often spend several hours a day scrolling through their feeds, posting pictures, and interacting with others online. They may experience negative consequences as a result of their social media use, such as neglecting work or school responsibilities, social isolation, and even physical health problems.

Signs and Symptoms of Social Media Addiction

Here are some of the signs and symptoms of social media addiction:

1. Constantly checking social media: Individuals who are addicted to social media may feel compelled to check their accounts frequently throughout the day, even during important activities or events.

2. Losing track of time: Social media addiction can cause individuals to lose track of time while using social media. This can lead to neglecting other important activities or responsibilities.

3. Withdrawal symptoms: Individuals who are addicted to social media may experience withdrawal symptoms such as irritability, anxiety, and restlessness when they are unable to access their social media accounts.

4. Neglecting responsibilities: Social media addiction can cause individuals to neglect important responsibilities such as work, school, or personal relationships.

5. Social isolation: Individuals who are addicted to social media may spend more time interacting with others online than in-person. This can lead to social isolation and a lack of real-world connections.

6. Physical health problems: Excessive social media use can lead to physical health problems such as eye strain, headaches, and poor sleep.

7. Mood changes: Individuals who are addicted to social media may experience mood changes such as depression, anxiety, or irritability when they are unable to access their social media accounts or when they receive negative feedback online.

Effects of Social Media Addiction

Social media addiction can have negative effects on a person's mental and physical health. Some of the effects of social media addiction include:

1. Depression and anxiety: Social media addiction can lead to feelings of depression and anxiety, particularly when individuals compare themselves to others on social media.

2. Poor sleep: Excessive social media use can disrupt sleep patterns, leading to poor sleep quality and insomnia.

3. Eye strain and headaches: Staring at a screen for long periods can cause eye strain and headaches.

4. Social isolation: Social media addiction can lead to social isolation and a lack of real-world connections.

5. Neglect of responsibilities: Individuals who are addicted to social media may neglect important responsibilities such as work, school, or personal relationships.

6. Reduced productivity: Social media addiction can reduce productivity and focus, leading to poor performance at work or school.

7. Financial problems: Social media addiction can lead to financial problems if individuals spend money on social media platforms or neglect work or business responsibilities.

Managing Social Media Addiction

If you suspect that you or someone you know is addicted to social media, there are several ways to manage the addiction. Here are some tips:

1. Limit social media use: Set a time limit for social media use and stick to it. Use apps or features that can help limit the time spent on social media.

2. Engage in real-world activities: Spend time engaging in real-world activities such as exercise, reading, or spending time with friends and family.

3. Seek professional help: If social media addiction is interfering with daily life, consider seeking professional help from a mental health professional.

4. Join support groups: Join support groups or online communities for individuals who are struggling with social media addiction. These groups can provide support and accountability.

5. Practice mindfulness: Mindfulness practices such as meditation or deep

breathing can help reduce the urge to use social media excessively.

6. Turn off notifications: Turn off social media notifications to reduce the urge to constantly check social media.

7. Create a schedule: Create a schedule that includes time for social media use and other important activities. Stick to the schedule to establish healthy habits.

Conclusion

Social media addiction is a growing concern that can have negative effects on a person's mental and physical health. It is important to recognize the signs and symptoms of social media addiction and take steps to manage it. By limiting social media use, engaging in real-world activities, seeking professional help, and practicing mindfulness, individuals can overcome social media addiction and live a healthier, more fulfilling life.

Chapter 4. Coping with FOMO (Fear of Missing Out) and Comparison Envy on Social Media

Introduction

Social media has become an integral part of our lives. It connects us with people from all around the world and provides us with easy access to a wealth of information. However, social media platforms have also given rise to a new set of challenges. One of the most prevalent challenges is FOMO (fear of missing out) and comparison envy.

FOMO is a feeling of anxiety or fear that one might miss out on something exciting or interesting happening on social media. Comparison envy, on the other hand, is a feeling of inferiority or dissatisfaction caused by comparing oneself to others on social media. These two feelings can cause a lot of stress, anxiety, and even depression. In this article, we will discuss coping strategies to deal with FOMO and comparison envy on social media.

Understanding FOMO and Comparison Envy

FOMO is the fear of missing out on something exciting or interesting happening on social media. Social media platforms are designed to create a sense of urgency and excitement by constantly updating content. This can make people feel like they are missing out on something important if they are not constantly checking their social media feeds.

Comparison envy, on the other hand, is the feeling of inferiority or dissatisfaction caused by comparing oneself to others on social media. Social media platforms are full of images and posts of people living their best lives, going on exotic vacations, attending glamorous events, and having fun with their friends. This can make people feel like they are not living their lives to the fullest or that they are not as happy or successful as others.

Both FOMO and comparison envy can have a negative impact on mental health. People who experience FOMO and comparison envy may feel stressed, anxious, or even depressed. It is essential to develop coping strategies to deal with these feelings and prevent them from taking over our lives.

Coping Strategies for FOMO and Comparison Envy

1. Take a break from social media

The first and most effective way to deal with FOMO and comparison envy is to take a break from social media. This means deleting social media apps from your phone, avoiding checking social media accounts, and limiting your social media use. Taking a break from social media can help you re-evaluate your priorities and focus on your own life without the distraction of other people's lives.

2. Cultivate gratitude

Cultivating gratitude is another effective way to deal with FOMO and comparison envy. Instead of focusing on what you don't have or what you are missing out on, focus on what you do have and what you are grateful for. Take some time each day to reflect on the things in your life that bring you joy and happiness.

3. Be mindful

Practicing mindfulness can also help you deal with FOMO and comparison envy. Mindfulness means being present in the moment and fully engaged in what you are doing. When you are mindful, you are less likely to compare yourself to others or feel like you are missing out on something.

4. Set realistic expectations

It is important to set realistic expectations for yourself when it comes to social media. Remember that social media is a highlight reel, and people only share the best parts of their lives. Don't compare yourself to others on social media, and don't set unrealistic expectations for yourself based on what you see on social media.

5. Connect with others

Connecting with others can help you feel less isolated and reduce feelings of FOMO and comparison envy. Join a group or club that interests you, volunteer, or reach out to friends and family. Real-life connections are often more meaningful than virtual connections, and they can help you feel more fulfilled and satisfied.

It is essential to focus on your own goals and priorities rather than comparing yourself to others. Make a list of your goals and work towards achieving them. Celebrate your own accomplishments and progress instead of comparing yourself to others. This will help you build your confidence and reduce the impact of FOMO and comparison envy on your mental health.

Taking care of yourself is important for both physical and mental health. Engage in activities that make you feel good, such as exercise, meditation, or reading a good book. Take time to relax and recharge, and prioritize self-care in your daily routine.

Limiting your social media use can help you reduce feelings of FOMO and comparison envy. Set a specific time each day to check your social media accounts and stick to it. Avoid checking social media first thing in the morning or before going to bed, as this can disrupt your sleep and increase feelings of anxiety.

Changing your perspective can help you deal with FOMO and comparison envy. Instead of feeling jealous or inferior to others, try to view social media as a source of inspiration or motivation. Look for positive and uplifting content that can inspire you to pursue your own goals and passions.

Conclusion

FOMO and comparison envy are common feelings experienced by many people on social media. They can have a negative impact on mental health and well-being. However, there are several coping strategies that can help you deal with these feelings and prevent them from taking over your life. Taking a break from social media, cultivating gratitude, practicing mindfulness, setting realistic expectations, connecting with others, focusing on your own goals, practicing self-care, limiting social media use, and changing your perspective can all help you manage FOMO and comparison envy. By developing these coping strategies, you can enjoy the benefits of social media while avoiding the negative impact on your mental health.

Introduction

Social media has become a ubiquitous part of our lives. From scrolling through our feeds during breakfast to checking our notifications before bed, we are constantly plugged in. While social media has many benefits, such as staying connected with loved ones and staying up-to-date on current events, it can also be a source of stress, anxiety, and even addiction. That's why it's essential to practice mindful social media use. In this article, we'll explore the importance of mindful social media use and how to incorporate it into your daily routine.

The Negative Effects of Mindless Social Media Use

Mindless social media use refers to scrolling through your feeds without intention or purpose. While it might seem harmless, mindless social media use can have negative effects on our mental health. Studies have shown that excessive social media use is linked to higher levels of depression, anxiety, and feelings of loneliness. Constantly comparing ourselves to others on social media can lead to feelings of inadequacy and low self-esteem. In addition, the addictive nature of social media can lead to decreased productivity, difficulty focusing, and a disrupted sleep schedule.

The Benefits of Mindful Social Media Use

On the other hand, mindful social media use can have many positive effects on our mental health. By being intentional with our social media use, we can reap the benefits of staying connected with loved ones, finding inspiration, and learning new things. Mindful social media use can also help us feel more present in our daily lives and less distracted by the constant stream of notifications. In addition, setting boundaries and limits on our social media use can lead to increased productivity and better sleep hygiene.

Tips for Practicing Mindful Social Media Use

So how can you incorporate mindful social media use into your daily routine? Here are some tips:

1. Set Intentions: Before opening your social media apps, take a moment to set an intention for your use. Ask yourself why you are using social media and what you hope to gain from it. This can help you stay focused and avoid getting lost in the endless scroll.

2. Schedule Time: Rather than checking social media throughout the day, try scheduling specific times to check your accounts. This can help you avoid getting distracted and increase your productivity.

3. Take Breaks: It's important to take breaks from social media regularly. Consider taking a day off from social media each week or taking short breaks throughout the day.

4. Unfollow or Mute: If you find that certain accounts or posts are causing you stress or anxiety, consider unfollowing or muting them. You don't need to see everything that's

posted on social media, and it's important to prioritize your mental health.

5. Be Present: When you're using social media, try to be fully present in the moment. Avoid multitasking or getting distracted by other tasks. By being fully present, you can enjoy the benefits of social media without feeling overwhelmed.

Conclusion

Mindful social media use is essential for maintaining our mental health and well-being. By setting intentions, scheduling time, taking breaks, unfollowing or muting, and being present, we can reap the benefits of social media without experiencing the negative effects. Remember to prioritize your mental health and make mindful social media use a part of your daily routine.

Chapter 6. Building and Maintaining Positive Relationships on Social Media

Introduction

Social media has revolutionized the way people interact and communicate with each other. It has become a crucial part of our daily lives, allowing us to connect with friends, family, and even strangers from different parts of the world. With billions of people using social media platforms such as Facebook, Instagram, Twitter, and LinkedIn, the possibilities for building and maintaining positive relationships are endless.

However, social media can also be a breeding ground for negativity, hatred, and misunderstandings, which can often lead to the breakdown of relationships. Therefore, it is essential to know how to build and maintain positive relationships on social media. In this article, we will discuss some tips and strategies for building and maintaining positive relationships on social media.

1. Be Authentic and Genuine

One of the keys to building and maintaining positive relationships on social media is to be authentic and genuine. People appreciate authenticity, and they can easily tell when someone is being fake or insincere. Therefore, it is important to be yourself and express your true thoughts and feelings.

When interacting with others on social media, try to be honest, transparent, and sincere. Don't pretend to be someone you're not or say things that you don't believe in just to impress others. Instead, be true to yourself and your values, and people will respect and appreciate you for it.

2. Listen and Respond

Another important aspect of building and maintaining positive relationships on social media is to listen and respond. Social media is a two-way conversation, and it's important to listen to what others have to say and respond appropriately.

When someone reaches out to you or comments on your posts, take the time to read and respond to their message. Show that you value their input and appreciate their efforts to connect with you. Respond in a friendly and respectful manner, and try to engage them in a meaningful conversation.

3. Be Positive and Constructive

Social media can be a breeding ground for negativity and hostility. However, if you want to build and maintain positive relationships, it's important to be positive and constructive in your interactions.

Instead of criticizing or attacking others, try to offer constructive feedback and suggestions. Focus on the positive aspects of a situation, and try to find common ground with others. By being positive and constructive, you can create a more welcoming and inclusive environment that fosters positive relationships.

4. Show Appreciation and Gratitude

Showing appreciation and gratitude is another important aspect of building and maintaining positive relationships on social media. When someone does something nice for you or shares something valuable, take the time to show your appreciation.

You can show appreciation by liking, commenting, or sharing their post, or by sending them a private message. You can also show gratitude by acknowledging their efforts publicly and thanking them for their contribution.

5. Engage in Meaningful Conversations

Engaging in meaningful conversations is another way to build and maintain positive relationships on social media. Instead of just liking or commenting on a post, try to start a meaningful conversation with the person.

Ask them questions, share your thoughts and experiences, and try to find common ground. By engaging in meaningful conversations, you can build a deeper connection with others and create a more positive and supportive community.

6. Be Respectful and Tolerant

Respect and tolerance are essential for building and maintaining positive relationships on social media. With so many different opinions and viewpoints, it's important to be respectful and tolerant of others' beliefs and perspectives.

If you disagree with someone, try to express your opinion in a respectful and constructive manner. Avoid personal attacks or insults, and try to find common ground. By being respectful and tolerant, you can create a more welcoming and inclusive environment that fosters positive relationships.

7. Set Boundaries and Limits

Finally, it's important to set boundaries and limits when building and maintaining positive relationships on social media. While social media can be a great tool for connecting with others, it can also be overwhelming and time-consuming.

Therefore, it's important to set boundaries and limits to ensure that social media doesn't consume your entire life. Set a schedule for checking your social media accounts, and stick to it. Don't feel obligated to respond to every message or comment immediately, and don't let social media interfere with your personal or professional life.

Conclusion

Social media has changed the way people interact and communicate with each other. With billions of people using social media platforms, it's easier than ever to build and maintain positive relationships.

However, social media can also be a breeding ground for negativity, hatred, and misunderstandings. Therefore, it's important to know how to build and maintain positive relationships on social media.

To build and maintain positive relationships on social media, it's important to be authentic and genuine, listen and respond, be positive and constructive, show appreciation and gratitude, engage in meaningful conversations, be respectful and tolerant, and set boundaries and limits.

By following these tips and strategies, you can create a more positive and supportive community on social media and build strong and lasting relationships with others. Remember that social media is just a tool, and it's up to you to use it in a positive and constructive way.

Introduction

Cyberbullying, also known as online harassment, is the use of technology to deliberately harass, humiliate, or threaten someone. This form of bullying has become increasingly prevalent with the rise of social media and other online platforms. Cyberbullying can cause significant harm to the victim's mental health, reputation, and overall well-being. In this article, we will discuss how to identify cyberbullying and what steps can be taken to combat it.

Identifying Cyberbullying

Cyberbullying can take many forms, including sending threatening or abusive messages, sharing embarrassing photos or videos, spreading rumors, and impersonating someone online. It can happen on social media platforms, messaging apps, forums, and even through email. The following are some signs that someone may be experiencing cyberbullying:

1. Change in behavior: The victim may become withdrawn, anxious, or depressed. They may avoid social situations, lose interest in activities they once enjoyed, or become more irritable.

2. Unexplained absences: The victim may miss school or work more frequently, or they may avoid going to places where they may encounter the bully.

3. Changes in online behavior: The victim may stop using social media or other online platforms, or they may change their username or delete their accounts.

4. Physical symptoms: The victim may experience headaches, stomachaches, or other physical symptoms as a result of the stress and anxiety caused by the cyberbullying.

5. Signs of distress: The victim may express feelings of sadness, hopelessness, or helplessness. They may talk about self-harm or suicide.

Combating Cyberbullying

If you or someone you know is experiencing cyberbullying, there are steps that can be taken to combat it. The following are some strategies that can be effective:

1. Report the bullying: Most social media platforms and other online services have reporting mechanisms in place for cyberbullying. Encourage the victim to report the behavior to the platform's administrators or to the police if the behavior is criminal.

2. Block the bully: Victims can block the bully's phone number, email address, or social media account to prevent further harassment.

3. Document the harassment: Victims should keep a record of any abusive messages, posts, or other forms of harassment they receive. This documentation can be helpful in reporting the bullying to authorities or in seeking legal action.

4. Seek support: Victims of cyberbullying should seek support from friends, family, or mental health professionals. Counseling can

be particularly helpful in dealing with the emotional impact of cyberbullying.

5. Practice good online hygiene: Encourage victims to practice good online hygiene by using strong passwords, not sharing personal information online, and avoiding interacting with people they do not know or trust.

Preventing Cyberbullying

Preventing cyberbullying requires a multifaceted approach. The following are some strategies that can be effective in preventing cyberbullying:

1. Education: Education is key in preventing cyberbullying. Schools and other organizations can provide education on the harmful effects of cyberbullying and how to prevent it. This education should also cover the legal consequences of cyberbullying.

2. Parental involvement: Parents can play an important role in preventing cyberbullying. They should monitor their children's online activities, talk to their children about cyberbullying, and encourage open communication about any concerns.

3. Role modeling: Adults can model positive online behavior for young people. They should avoid engaging in cyberbullying or other negative online behaviors.

4. Encourage empathy: Encouraging empathy can help prevent cyberbullying. Children should be taught to consider the feelings of others and to treat others with kindness and respect.

5. Foster a positive online environment: Schools and other organizations can foster a positive online environment by promoting positive interactions, enforcing policies against cyberbullying, and providing resources for victims of cyberbullying.

Legal Consequences of Cyberbullying

Cyberbullying can have serious legal consequences. In many jurisdictions, cyberbullying is considered a crime, and perpetrators can face fines, imprisonment, or other legal penalties. The following are some legal consequences of cyberbullying:

1. Criminal charges: Cyberbullying can result in criminal charges, including harassment, stalking, and cyberstalking.

2. Civil lawsuits: Victims of cyberbullying can sue their bullies for damages, including emotional distress, loss of income, and medical expenses.

3. School disciplinary action: Schools can discipline students who engage in cyberbullying, including suspension or expulsion.

Conclusion

Cyberbullying is a serious problem that can have significant effects on the victim's mental health, reputation, and overall well-being. It is important to identify cyberbullying and take steps to combat it. Victims should report the bullying, block the bully, document the harassment, seek support, and practice good online hygiene. Preventing cyberbullying requires a multifaceted approach, including education, parental involvement, role modeling, encouraging empathy, and fostering a positive online environment. Cyberbullying can have serious legal consequences, including criminal charges, civil lawsuits, and school disciplinary action. By working together, we can combat cyberbullying and create a safer online environment for all.

Introduction

In today's digital age, social media has become a part and parcel of our lives. From Facebook to Twitter to Instagram, these platforms have transformed the way we communicate, share information, and connect with others. However, as much as social media has brought convenience and socialization, it also poses significant risks to our privacy and security. With the rise of cyber threats, identity theft, and data breaches, it has become crucial to take measures to protect ourselves while using these platforms. In this article, we will discuss some of the ways to safeguard your privacy and security on social media.

Create Strong and Unique Passwords

One of the most basic yet crucial steps to protect your social media accounts is to create strong and unique passwords. Weak passwords are easy to guess or crack, making it easier for hackers to gain access to your accounts. Therefore, it is recommended to use a combination of upper and lower case letters, numbers, and symbols when creating a password. Additionally, avoid using personal information such as your name, date of birth, or phone number, as they are easy to guess. Furthermore, it is crucial to have a unique password for each social media account to prevent hackers from gaining access to all your accounts if one is compromised.

Enable Two-Factor Authentication

Two-factor authentication is an additional security layer that requires users to provide two forms of identification to access their accounts. This authentication process adds an extra layer of security, making it harder for hackers to gain access to your accounts. Therefore, it is recommended to enable two-factor authentication on all your social media accounts. You can set up two-factor authentication by adding your phone number, email address, or a third-party authentication app that generates a unique code to access your accounts.

Review and Adjust Privacy Settings

Social media platforms provide users with privacy settings that allow them to control who can see their posts, profile, and personal information. Therefore, it is essential to review and adjust your privacy settings regularly to ensure that you are only sharing information with people you trust. You can adjust your privacy settings by going to the platform's settings or privacy tab, where you can select who can see your posts, photos, and other personal information. Moreover, you can also limit the amount of personal information you share on your profile, such as your location, date of birth, or phone number.

Be Cautious of Suspicious Messages and Links

Phishing attacks are prevalent on social media, where hackers use fake accounts and messages to lure users into clicking on malicious links or downloading harmful software. Therefore, it is essential to be cautious of suspicious messages and links that you receive on social media platforms. If you receive a message from an unknown person or an unsolicited message, do not click on any links or download any files, as they may contain malware or viruses. Moreover, avoid sharing any personal information or financial information with anyone on social media platforms.

Avoid Public Wi-Fi

Public Wi-Fi networks are often unsecured, making it easier for hackers to intercept your data and gain access to your social media accounts. Therefore, it is recommended to avoid using public Wi-Fi networks when accessing your social media accounts. If you have to use a public Wi-Fi network, ensure that you are connected to a secure and reliable network that requires a password or a security key.

Update Software and Apps Regularly

Social media platforms and apps release updates regularly to fix security vulnerabilities and improve performance. Therefore, it is essential to update your social media apps and software regularly to ensure that you have the latest security patches and features. Moreover, ensure that you have antivirus software installed on your device to protect against malware and viruses.

Conclusion

Social media has transformed the way we communicate and share information with others. However, it also poses significant risks to our privacy and security. Therefore, it is crucial to take measures to protect ourselves while using these platforms. By creating strong and unique passwords, enabling two-factor authentication, reviewing and adjusting privacy settings, being cautious of suspicious messages and links, avoiding public Wi-Fi, and updating software and apps regularly, we can safeguard our privacy and security on social media. It is essential to remain vigilant and mindful of the information we share on these platforms, as our online presence can have a significant impact on our personal and professional lives. Ultimately, taking these steps can help us enjoy the benefits of social media while mitigating the risks associated with using it.

Introduction

In today's world, social media has become an integral part of our daily lives. It has revolutionized the way we interact with people, get information, and even conduct business. However, the overuse of social media can lead to negative effects on our mental and emotional well-being. That's why it's essential to find a balance between using social media and other aspects of our lives, such as work, family, and personal growth. In this article, we'll explore the importance of setting boundaries and time management when it comes to using social media.

Why Do We Need to Set Boundaries and Manage Time for Social Media?

Social media can easily consume a significant amount of our time and attention, leading to negative consequences. For instance, excessive use of social media can lead to addiction, poor sleep quality, anxiety, and depression. It can also affect our productivity, social skills, and even our relationships. That's why it's crucial to set boundaries and manage our time when it comes to using social media.

Setting boundaries means defining what's acceptable and what's not when it comes to social media use. It involves establishing limits on the amount of time and energy we spend on social media, the types of content we consume, and the people we interact with. On the other hand, time management involves planning and prioritizing our activities to ensure that we use our time effectively and efficiently. It means allocating time for social media use and balancing it with other essential activities.

Let's explore some tips on how to set boundaries and manage our time when it comes to social media use.

1. Define Your Goals and Priorities

The first step in setting boundaries and managing time for social media is to define your goals and priorities. What do you want to achieve by using social media? Is it for personal growth, networking, or entertainment? What other activities are essential to you, such as work, family, or hobbies? Once you have identified your goals and priorities, you can set limits on your social media use accordingly.

For instance, if you use social media for work, you may need to spend more time on it than if you use it for personal entertainment. If spending time with your family is a priority, you may need to limit your social media use during family time. By setting your goals and priorities, you can determine how much time and energy you should allocate to social media.

2. Set Limits on Your Social Media Use

Once you have defined your goals and priorities, the next step is to set limits on your social media use. You can start by determining how much time you should spend on social media daily, weekly, or monthly. You can also set boundaries on the types of content you consume, the people you interact with, and the platforms you use.

For instance, you can limit your social media use to certain times of the day, such as before or after work, or during lunch breaks. You can also use apps that help you monitor your social media use, such as StayFocused or RescueTime. These apps allow you to set time limits on your social media use and alert you when you've reached your limit.

3. Practice Digital Detox

Another effective way to set boundaries and manage time for social media use is to practice digital detox. Digital detox involves taking a break from technology, including social media, to focus on other essential aspects of our lives. It means disconnecting from social media for a certain period, such as a day, a weekend, or a week.

Digital detox can help you recharge and reconnect with yourself, your family, and your surroundings. It can also improve your productivity, creativity, and mental clarity. To practice digital detox, you can turn off your phone or computer for a certain period or use apps that help you stay offline, such as Offtime or Freedom.

4. Create a Schedule

Creating a schedule is another effective way to manage your time and set boundaries for social media use. A schedule helps you plan and prioritize your activities, including social media use. It ensures that you allocate enough time for other essential activities and that you don't spend too much time on social media.

When creating a schedule, you can allocate a certain amount of time for social media use, depending on your goals and priorities. For instance, you can allocate 30 minutes per day for checking social media or 2 hours per week for creating social media content. You can also set specific times for social media use, such as early morning, lunchtime, or evening.

5. Be Mindful of Your Social Media Use

Being mindful of your social media use means being aware of your emotions, thoughts, and behaviors when using social media. It means paying attention to how social media affects your mood, productivity, and relationships. By being mindful, you can identify when social media use becomes excessive or harmful and take steps to reduce it.

To be mindful of your social media use, you can ask yourself the following questions:

- ➢ How do I feel after using social media?
- ➢ Is social media affecting my productivity or concentration?
- ➢ Am I using social media to avoid other important tasks or emotions?
- ➢ Is social media affecting my relationships or social skills?
- ➢ Am I comparing myself to others on social media?

By asking these questions, you can identify the negative effects of social media use and take steps to reduce them.

Conclusion

Setting boundaries and managing time for social media use is essential for our mental and emotional well-being. By defining our goals and priorities, setting limits on social media use, practicing digital detox, creating a schedule, and being mindful of our social media use, we can achieve a healthy balance between social media and other aspects of our lives. It's important to remember that social media is a tool that can enhance our lives if used in moderation and with intention.

Introduction

In today's world, social media platforms have become an integral part of our daily lives. From checking notifications and scrolling through feeds to constantly checking updates, it's easy to become immersed in the digital world. However, spending too much time on social media can have a negative impact on our mental and emotional well-being. Therefore, it's important to take breaks from social media to reconnect with the real world and experience its benefits.

The negative impacts of social media

Social media has been associated with several negative effects, including anxiety, depression, and loneliness. Studies have shown that excessive use of social media can lead to feelings of envy, low self-esteem, and even addictive behavior.

Additionally, social media can also create unrealistic expectations, and contribute to a constant need for validation.

Moreover, social media platforms are designed to keep users engaged for as long as possible, leading to excessive screen time and less time spent on meaningful interactions with loved ones. This can lead to feelings of disconnection from the real world, and exacerbate mental health problems.

The benefits of taking breaks from social media

Disconnecting from social media can have a range of benefits for our mental and emotional well-being. Here are some of the key benefits:

1. Improved mental health

Several studies have shown that social media use is linked to higher levels of anxiety and depression. Taking a break from social media can reduce these negative effects and improve overall mental health. By disconnecting from social media, individuals can focus on self-care and engage in activities that promote well-being, such as meditation, exercise, and spending time in nature.

2. Better quality relationships

Excessive use of social media can lead to a sense of disconnection from loved ones. Taking a break from social media can help individuals to reconnect with family and friends, and spend more quality time together. By engaging in face-to-face interactions, individuals can deepen their relationships and create lasting memories.

3. Increased productivity

Social media can be a major distraction, often leading to decreased productivity and concentration. Taking a break from social media can help individuals to focus on important tasks and increase their productivity. By eliminating digital distractions, individuals can improve their ability to concentrate, and achieve more in less time.

4. Enhanced creativity

Social media platforms can be a source of inspiration, but they can also stifle creativity by limiting the ability to think outside the box. By disconnecting from social media, individuals can engage in activities that promote creativity, such as painting, writing, or playing an instrument. This can lead to a renewed sense of inspiration and a fresh perspective on life.

5. Improved self-esteem

Social media can create unrealistic expectations and contribute to a constant need for validation. Taking a break from social media can help individuals to focus on self-care, and develop a more positive self-image. By engaging in activities that promote self-esteem, such as exercise and meditation, individuals can boost their confidence and feel more comfortable in their own skin.

Tips for disconnecting from social media

If you're ready to take a break from social media, here are some tips to help you get started:

1. Set goals and boundaries

Before disconnecting from social media, set clear goals and boundaries. Decide how long you want to take a break for, and what activities you want to engage in during that time. Additionally, set boundaries around when and how often you will use social media once you return.

2. Remove social media apps from your phone

To reduce temptation, consider removing social media apps from your phone. This can help you to avoid mindlessly scrolling through feeds, and make it easier to disconnect from the digital world.

3. Find alternative activities

To make the most of your time away from social media, find alternative activities that promote well-being, such as reading, exercising, or spending time in nature. By engaging in activities that you enjoy and that make you feel good, you'll be less likely to miss social media.

If you're taking an extended break from social media, it can be helpful to let your contacts know. Send a message to friends and family, letting them know that you're taking a break and will be less available online. This can help to reduce the pressure to stay connected, and give you the space you need to recharge.

Disconnecting from social media can be challenging, especially if you're used to checking your phone constantly. To help ease the transition, practice mindfulness techniques, such as deep breathing or meditation. By focusing on the present moment, you can reduce feelings of anxiety or restlessness, and feel more grounded.

Conclusion

Social media can have a negative impact on our mental and emotional well-being. While it's tempting to stay connected online, it's important to take breaks from social media to reconnect with the real world and experience its benefits. By disconnecting from social media, individuals can improve their mental health, deepen their relationships, increase productivity, boost creativity, and enhance their self-esteem. With the right mindset and strategies, taking a break from social media can be a transformative experience that helps you to live a happier and more fulfilling life.

Introduction

Social media has become an integral part of our daily lives. It allows us to connect with friends, family, and even coworkers. However, as social media has grown in popularity, so has its impact on the workplace. Navigating social media in the workplace can be a tricky task, as it requires a balance between personal expression and professional etiquette. In this article, we will discuss best practices and etiquette for navigating social media in the workplace.

1. Understand Your Company's Social Media Policy

Before you start posting, it's important to understand your company's social media policy. This policy outlines the expectations and guidelines for employees when it comes to social media use. Some companies have strict policies that prohibit employees from mentioning the company or sharing any information about the company on social media. Other companies encourage employees to engage with social media and promote the company's brand.

Understanding your company's social media policy can help you navigate the do's and don'ts of social media in the workplace. Make sure to read the policy thoroughly and ask questions if anything is unclear.

2. Keep Personal and Professional Accounts Separate

It's important to keep your personal and professional accounts separate. Your personal social media accounts are a reflection of your personal life, and your professional accounts are a reflection of your professional life. Blurring the lines between the two can lead to confusion and potential conflicts of interest.

When using social media in the workplace, make sure to use your professional account. This account should be used for work-related posts, such as company news and updates. Your personal account should be used for personal posts, such as photos of your family and friends.

3. Be Mindful of What You Post

When using social media in the workplace, it's important to be mindful of what you post. Your posts can have a significant impact on your professional reputation, so it's important to think before you post. Avoid posting anything that could be considered offensive or inappropriate, such as discriminatory comments or photos of you engaging in illegal activities.

Additionally, be mindful of how your posts could reflect on your company. Avoid posting anything that could be perceived as negative or critical of your company, even if it's your personal opinion. Remember, your social media presence is a reflection of your professional reputation.

4. Don't Engage in Online Arguments

It's important to avoid engaging in online arguments on social media, especially when it comes to work-related issues. Online arguments can quickly escalate and can damage relationships with coworkers and clients. If you have an issue with someone, it's best to address it in person or through a private message.

If you do find yourself in an online argument, try to remain calm and professional. Avoid using inflammatory language or personal attacks. Remember, social media is a public platform, and your behavior can have an impact on your professional reputation.

5. Respect Confidentiality and Privacy

When using social media in the workplace, it's important to respect confidentiality and privacy. Avoid sharing any confidential or proprietary information about your company or coworkers. This includes financial information, customer data, and trade secrets.

Additionally, respect the privacy of your coworkers. Avoid posting photos or personal information about your coworkers without their permission. If you're unsure if something is appropriate to post, err on the side of caution and ask for permission.

6. Be Authentic and Genuine

While it's important to be mindful of what you post on social media, it's also important to be authentic and genuine. Authenticity and genuineness can help you build trust with your coworkers and clients.

When posting on social media, try to showcase your personality and interests. Share your hobbies and passions, and engage with others who share similar interests. This can help you build connections with your coworkers and clients outside of work.

7. Monitor Your Social Media Presence

Finally, it's important to monitor your social media presence. Set up notifications for any mentions of your company or your name on social media. This can help you stay informed of any conversations happening about your company and can allow you to address any issues that arise.

Additionally, regularly review your social media profiles to ensure that they accurately reflect your professional image. Remove any posts or comments that could be perceived as negative or unprofessional.

Conclusion

Navigating social media in the workplace requires a balance between personal expression and professional etiquette. By understanding your company's social media policy, keeping personal and professional accounts separate, being mindful of what you post, avoiding online arguments, respecting confidentiality and privacy, being authentic and genuine, and monitoring your social media presence, you can effectively use social media in the workplace while maintaining a positive professional reputation. Remember, your social media presence is a reflection of your professional image, so it's important to be thoughtful and deliberate in your social media use.

"Social Media Madness: How to Maintain Your Sanity in a Digital World" is an insightful guide that explores the impact of social media on mental health and well-being. The book comprises eleven chapters that address different aspects of social media usage, including addiction, FOMO, cyberbullying, and privacy concerns. The first chapter sets the tone for the book, providing an introduction to the phenomenon of social media madness and its prevalence in today's world. The subsequent chapters delve deeper into the various challenges posed by social media and provide practical strategies for mitigating their negative effects. By drawing on current research, this book offers a comprehensive approach to achieving a healthy relationship with social media that allows readers to thrive in both their personal and professional lives.

ABOUT THE AUTHOR

Mr. C. P. Kumar is a retired Scientist 'G' from the National Institute of Hydrology, Roorkee, Uttarakhand, India. With a wealth of experience in his field, he has also been practicing alternative healing therapies for several years. He is skilled in Reiki Healing and Chakra Balancing with Pendulum Dowsing, and offers holistic therapy through Emotional Freedom Technique (EFT) for emotional issues. You can email Mr. Kumar at cpkumar@yahoo.com and also visit his Reiki blog at https://reiki-roorkee.blogspot.com/ for more information.

www.ingramcontent.com/pod-product-compliance
Lightning Source LLC
Chambersburg PA
CBHW051810130726

47987CB00003B/1201